THE CLEOPATRA EFFECT

*Embracing the Power
of Ancient Wisdom*

The information contained within this document is provided for educational and entertainment purposes only. While every effort has been made to present accurate, up-to-date, reliable, and complete information, no warranties of any kind, either express or implied, are made. Readers acknowledge that the author is not providing legal, financial, medical, or professional advice. The content of this book has been compiled from various sources. Before attempting any techniques described in this book, please consult with a licensed professional.

Contents

Chapter 1: The Allure of Cleopatra: The Echoes of a Timeless Legacy

The name Cleopatra conjures a spectrum of images: a ruler, a seductress, a diplomat, and a scholar. Beyond her portrayal as a figure entangled in the political dynamics of ancient Rome, Cleopatra VII of Egypt stands as a testament to the enduring power of influence and intelligence. Her legacy, shrouded in both mystique and historical significance, serves not merely as a tale of sovereignty and seduction but as a reservoir of timeless wisdom relevant even in today's fast-paced world.

Cleopatra: The Woman Behind the Myth

To fully embrace the lessons of Cleopatra's life, one must first understand the woman behind the centuries-old myths. Born into the Ptolemaic dynasty in 69 BC, a lineage of Greek origin that ruled Egypt after Alexander the Great's death, Cleopatra ascended to the throne at the tender age of 18. Her early reign was marked by a blend of tumult and ambition, navigating through a labyrinth of political intrigue and family betrayal. Unlike her predecessors, Cleopatra was a polyglot who spoke several languages and was the first of her line to learn Egyptian, which she used to deepen her connection with her subjects and solidify her power.

Intelligence and Charm: Tools of Trade

Cleopatra's intelligence was a cornerstone of her rule. She was educated by the best tutors in mathematics, philosophy, oratory, and astronomy. This education not only prepared her for the complexities of her role but also equipped her with the strategic acumen that characterized her political and romantic alliances. Cleopatra's charm and intelligence were such that she could engage the likes of Julius Caesar and Mark Antony, not merely as lovers but as political allies. This aspect of her life highlights a crucial lesson: the power of intellect and charisma as tools for navigating both personal and professional landscapes.

The Symbolism of Cleopatra's Allure

The allure of Cleopatra also lay in her mastery of symbolism. She famously presented herself as the reincarnation of the goddess Isis, skillfully intertwining her identity with divine authority. This not only strengthened her appeal but also solidified her status as a demi-goddess in the eyes of her people, thereby legitimizing her rule in a politically tumultuous era. The symbolism extended beyond her persona; it was woven into her public appearances, her dress, and her conduct, each element carefully crafted to communicate power and divine favor.

Embracing Cleopatra's Wisdom Today

In our modern era, where leadership often demands a blend of charisma, knowledge, and strategic communication, Cleopatra's life offers rich lessons. She exemplifies how personal branding and the adept use of symbols can enhance one's influence and authority. In a world dominated by digital communication and global connectivity, understanding the power behind symbols—whether they be personal branding on social media or corporate branding in business—can be as critical as it was in the courts of ancient Alexandria.

Meditation: Visualizing Cleopatra's Royal Court

Let us engage in a brief meditation to connect more deeply with the essence of Cleopatra's power. Close your eyes and breathe deeply. Imagine yourself walking through the grand halls of Cleopatra's palace in Alexandria. The walls are adorned with intricate hieroglyphs, each telling stories of gods and goddesses. The air is fragrant with incense, and soft light filters through linen curtains, casting gentle patterns on the marble floor.

As you walk, you approach the throne room. Cleopatra sits upon her golden throne, her presence commanding yet graceful. She wears a flowing robe of royal blue and a crown that symbolizes her divine right to rule. Her eyes meet yours, and in them, you see a spark of the formidable intelligence and charisma that guided her through tumultuous times.

Cleopatra gestures for you to come closer. As you approach, she speaks of the burdens of leadership and the importance of wisdom and courage. Her words inspire you to reflect on your own life and the areas where you can apply her ancient wisdom. Take another deep breath and carry with you a sense of empowerment, a gift from the past, as you slowly open your eyes and return to the present.

The allure of Cleopatra is not merely in her story but in what her story represents: the profound impact of intellectual and personal power. As we move through this book, let each chapter draw you deeper into the practical applications of her life's lessons, enabling you to harness a fraction of her legendary prowess in your daily life. Whether you seek to enhance your leadership skills, expand your intellectual horizons, or cultivate a charismatic presence, Cleopatra's legacy offers a blueprint for greatness that transcends the boundaries of time.

Chapter 2: Leadership Inspired by the Queen

Cleopatra VII, the last active ruler of the Ptolemaic Kingdom of Egypt, has left behind a legacy that has transcended centuries. Her reign is not just a tale of power and seduction but a masterclass in leadership, negotiation, and governance. In this chapter, we delve into the essence of Cleopatra's leadership style and explore how modern leaders can draw inspiration from her strategies to enhance their own capabilities.

The Essence of Cleopatra's Leadership

Cleopatra's approach to leadership was multifaceted, involving astute political acumen, personal charisma, and a deep understanding of power dynamics. She was not merely a figurehead; she was a strategist who actively engaged with her allies and adversaries alike.

Her leadership was characterized by a blend of boldness and subtlety—a duality that today's leaders can learn from.

Strategic Alliances

One of the hallmarks of Cleopatra's reign was her ability to form strategic alliances. Her liaisons with Julius Caesar and Mark Antony were not just romantic encounters but calculated political moves to strengthen her position against her rivals. Today's leaders can take a leaf out of her book by recognizing the importance of strategic partnerships in achieving business goals. It's about understanding the mutual benefits and fostering relationships that go beyond mere transactions.

Visionary Leadership

Cleopatra was a visionary who could see beyond the immediate political landscape to the possibilities that lay ahead. She reimagined Egypt's role in a rapidly changing world dominated by Roman power. Modern leaders should emulate her ability to look ahead and craft visions that inspire and mobilize their teams, especially in times of uncertainty. Visionary leadership involves anticipating future trends and preparing organizations to adapt and thrive.

Resilience in Adversity

Cleopatra's reign was riddled with challenges, from familial betrayals to the threat of annexation by Rome. Yet, her resilience in the face of adversity was remarkable. She was dethroned more than once, only to regain power through sheer determination and strategic maneuvering. For today's leaders, resilience is just as critical. The business world is volatile, and the ability to bounce back from setbacks is invaluable. Leaders must cultivate resilience, ensuring their organizations can withstand and emerge stronger from crises.

Cleopatra's Communication Mastery

Cleopatra was known for her eloquence and persuasive skills. She was fluent in several languages, which not only allowed her to communicate effectively but also to connect with people from different cultures and backgrounds. Modern leaders must recognize the power of communication—how it can bridge gaps, foster understanding, and build trust within and across teams.

Authenticity and Charisma

Cleopatra's charisma was legendary. It stemmed from her authenticity and the genuine interest she showed in others, regardless of their status. Authentic leadership fosters a positive organizational culture and builds loyalty. Leaders today can enhance their charisma by being more approachable, listening actively, and showing empathy.

Leadership by Example

Cleopatra led from the front, be it in diplomacy, battle, or administration. She was deeply involved in the governance of Egypt, demonstrating a commitment to her country and its people. Leadership by example is a powerful way to instill confidence and motivate others. Leaders who are willing to do what they ask of others earn respect and dedication.

Decision-Making with Wisdom

Cleopatra's decisions, whether engaging in warfare or forming political alliances, were marked by a blend of intuition and wisdom. She understood the importance of timely and decisive action. Effective leadership involves making informed decisions swiftly and confidently, which today can be supported by data and analytics but should also include an intuitive understanding of human behavior and market dynamics.

Meditation: Reflecting on Personal Leadership Qualities

Let us now take a moment to engage in a meditative practice that Cleopatra herself might have appreciated in times of solitude and reflection.

Meditation Guide:

Find a Quiet Place: Sit comfortably in a quiet space where you won't be disturbed.

Breathe and Relax: Close your eyes. Take deep, slow breaths to relax your mind and body.

13

Visualize: Imagine yourself walking through the bustling streets of ancient Alexandria. Feel the warm breeze and hear the sounds of the marketplace.

Meet Cleopatra: Visualize meeting Cleopatra in her royal palace. Notice her demeanor, her confidence, and the respect she commands.

Reflect on Your Leadership: Think about your own leadership style. What qualities do you share with Cleopatra? What areas could you improve?

Seek Guidance: In your visualization, ask Cleopatra for advice on a current challenge you face as a leader.

Listen and Learn: Listen to her words and take to heart the wisdom she shares.

Return: Gradually bring your awareness back to the present. Open your eyes when you're ready.

Cleopatra's legacy as a leader is not just about the power she wielded but about the strategic, resilient, and charismatic way in which she led. By integrating some of Cleopatra's leadership traits, modern leaders can enhance their effectiveness and inspire their teams to achieve greater successes. Embrace the challenges and opportunities with the same vigor and wisdom as Cleopatra, and watch the transformation in your leadership journey unfold.

Chapter 3: The Art of Diplomacy

Cleopatra VII, the last active ruler of the Ptolemaic Kingdom of Egypt, remains one of the most renowned figures in history, not only for her compelling allure and dramatic life story but also for her shrewd diplomatic acumen. Cleopatra's reign was marked by political turmoil and societal upheavals, yet she navigated these with a sophistication and strategic finesse that remain instructive today. This chapter explores Cleopatra's diplomatic strategies and how modern individuals can apply these age-old tactics to contemporary challenges.

Diplomacy as an Art Form

For Cleopatra, diplomacy was more than a mere tool of statecraft; it was an art form. Her reign required a delicate balancing act: she needed to secure her throne, manage relationships with Roman powers, and maintain the prosperity of Egypt. Each of these tasks demanded a masterful use of diplomacy. Cleopatra's approach emphasized the importance of personal charm, intelligence, and the ability to read and influence others—a skill set equally valuable in today's world.

Cultivating Charisma and Intellect

Cleopatra famously seduced two of the most powerful Roman figures of her time—Julius Caesar and Mark Antony. While often romanticized, these relationships were strategic masterstrokes in her diplomatic playbook. Cleopatra's charisma was backed by her sharp intellect; she was educated by Philostratus and spoke multiple languages fluently, which allowed her to negotiate directly without interpreters. Today, charisma and intellect remain potent tools in negotiation. Enhancing one's knowledge base and interpersonal skills can transform interactions in both professional and personal spheres.

Building Strategic Alliances

Cleopatra's alliances with Rome were crucial. They were not born out of mere affection but were strategic moves to strengthen her position against internal and external threats. In the modern context, strategic alliances are vital in business, politics, and social settings. Like Cleopatra, modern leaders must identify and cultivate relationships that will mutually benefit each party and advance their objectives.

Adapting to Changing Circumstances

Cleopatra's ability to adapt to rapidly changing political landscapes was another hallmark of her diplomacy. After Caesar's assassination, she quickly aligned with Mark Antony, understanding that her survival depended on Rome's support. In today's fast-paced world, adaptability is crucial. The ability to pivot strategies in response to new information and altered circumstances can mark the difference between success and failure.

Leveraging Symbolism and Perception

Cleopatra often used symbolism to her advantage, famously presenting herself as the reincarnation of the goddess Isis. This not only solidified her divine status among Egyptians but also played into the Roman fascination with exotic cultures, enhancing her allure and perceived power. Modern leaders can learn from Cleopatra's use of symbolism and perception management. Whether it's a brand's image in the marketplace or an individual's personal branding in their career, how one is perceived can significantly impact their influence and effectiveness.

Practicing Patience and Timing

Patience was another critical component of Cleopatra's diplomatic strategy. She knew when to press her advantage and when to retreat. Her timing in forming relationships with powerful Roman generals when they were most advantageous is a testament to her strategic patience. In today's world, timing can be everything—knowing when to launch a product, propose a partnership, or enter a new market can determine long-term success.

Meditation: Reflecting on Diplomatic Strengths

Meditation Exercise:

Find a Quiet Space: Begin by finding a quiet and comfortable place to sit or lie down.

Breathe and Relax: Close your eyes and take deep, slow breaths. With each exhale, let go of any tension in your body.

Visualize a Diplomatic Encounter: Imagine yourself in a grand, ancient Egyptian hall, facing a challenging diplomatic scenario. You are at the negotiating table with important figures whose alliances are crucial for your success.

Channel Cleopatra: Visualize yourself embodying Cleopatra's qualities—her charisma, intelligence, and strategic acumen. Feel her confidence and diplomatic grace infusing your being.

Negotiate: In your visualization, engage in the negotiation. Use thoughtful dialogue, pay attention to the body language of your counterparts, and strategically employ your knowledge and charm to sway the discussion in your favor.

Reflect: As the meditation ends, slowly bring yourself back to the present. Reflect on the qualities you embodied in your visualization. Consider how you can apply these traits in your real-life interactions to enhance your diplomatic effectiveness.

Cleopatra's legacy as a diplomat offers timeless lessons that can be applied to modern-day challenges. By studying her life and strategies, one can learn the importance of intellect, charisma, strategic alliances, adaptability, symbolism, and timing in negotiation and relationship management. Emulating Cleopatra's diplomatic tactics may empower modern individuals to navigate their worlds with similar grace and effectiveness.

Chapter 4: Beauty Secrets of the Ancient World

Cleopatra VII, the last active ruler of the Ptolemaic Kingdom of Egypt, remains an enduring symbol of beauty and allure centuries after her reign. Her sophisticated knowledge of cosmetics and personal care, woven deeply into her identity and political persona, offers timeless beauty secrets that modern individuals can adapt for their own wellness and self-care routines.

The Basis of Cleopatra's Beauty Regimen

Cleopatra's beauty regimen was not solely about enhancing physical appearance; it was intrinsically linked to her health, well-being, and even her political influence. She utilized natural resources, available from the fertile Nile Valley, incorporating ingredients like honey, aloe vera, and almond oil into her skincare. These substances, rich in vitamins and moisturizing properties, highlight a holistic approach to beauty, emphasizing nourishment and protection of the skin.

Cleopatra's Skincare Rituals

Milk and Honey Baths

One of the most famous aspects of Cleopatra's beauty routine was her legendary milk and honey baths. These baths were not mere indulgences; they had a practical purpose. Milk contains lactic acid, an alpha hydroxy acid that exfoliates the skin, removing dead skin cells and speeding up cell renewal. Honey is a natural humectant that moisturizes, soothes, and antibacterial, ideal for achieving a glowing complexion.

DIY Milk and Honey Bath:

Combine 2 cups of whole milk or milk powder with 1/2 cup of raw honey.

Dissolve the honey in warm milk and add it to a bath of lukewarm water.

Soak for 20 to 30 minutes, then rinse off with clean water.

Almond Oil Infusions

Cleopatra was also known to use almond oil as a base for fragrant infusions. Almond oil is naturally rich in vitamin E, which provides intense hydration and helps to protect skin from damage caused by UV radiation and oxidative stress.

Simple Almond Oil Moisturizer:

Mix a few drops of essential oil (like lavender or rose) with almond oil.

Apply to the face and body as a moisturizer.

Hair Care Secrets

Cleopatra's hair was said to be lush and radiant, adorned with jewels and intricate styles that signified her status. Her hair care routine likely included oils and plant extracts to keep her hair strong and shiny.

Aloe Vera Hair Mask:

Extract fresh aloe vera gel from the leaf of an aloe plant.

Apply the gel directly to the scalp and hair, leave it on for an hour, then rinse.

This treatment can soothe the scalp, condition the hair, and enhance natural shine.

Cleopatra's Use of Cosmetics

Cleopatra's use of makeup went beyond aesthetic enhancement; it was a tool for expressing sovereignty and divine status. She is famed for her dramatic eye makeup, which not only protected her eyes from the sun but also had spiritual significance.

Kohl Eyeliner

The dark eyeliner, or kohl, that Cleopatra used was made from ground minerals, including galena (lead sulfide) and malachite. Today, for health reasons, similar effects can be achieved using safer, modern eyeliners.

Modern Kohl Application:

Use a soft, black eyeliner to line both the upper and lower eyelids liberally.

Extend the line slightly at the corners to create Cleopatra's signature almond eye shape.

Dietary Contributions to Beauty

Cleopatra's diet also contributed to her radiant skin and overall health. Her meals likely included a bounty of fresh fruits, vegetables, and whole grains—all rich in vitamins and antioxidants, which are known today to combat aging and promote health.

Incorporating Cleopatra's Diet:

Include foods like pomegranates, figs, and grapes, which are high in antioxidants.

Eat a balanced diet with a good mix of protein, healthy fats, and carbohydrates for overall health and skin vitality.

Embracing Cleopatra's Beauty Secrets Today

While we might not live like a queen, we can still take inspiration from Cleopatra's beauty secrets to enhance our own routines. By incorporating natural ingredients into our skincare, adopting thoughtful dietary habits, and understanding the holistic nature of beauty, we can achieve a regal aura and timeless allure. These ancient practices remind us that beauty is not just about looking good but about cultivating a deeper sense of well-being and confidence.

Meditation: Connecting with Inner Beauty

To close this chapter, let us engage in a short meditation that embodies Cleopatra's approach to beauty— focusing not just on the exterior but on inner wellness and peace.

Guided Meditation:

Find a comfortable, quiet place to sit or recline.

Close your eyes and take several deep, calming breaths.

Visualize yourself seated by the banks of the Nile, the gentle sounds of water and nature around you.

Imagine a golden light enveloping you, symbolizing the nourishment and care you give your body and spirit.

Feel the warmth of this light as you remind yourself of your unique beauty, both inside and out.

Hold this image for a few moments, then gently bring your awareness back to the present.

Cleopatra's beauty secrets offer more than just ways to enhance physical appearance; they provide a blueprint for holistic living and wellness that is just as relevant in today's world as it was in ancient times.

Chapter 5: The Power of Knowledge

Cleopatra VII, the last active ruler of the Ptolemaic Kingdom of Egypt, remains a figure shrouded in myth and legend. Known for her breathtaking beauty and deadly alliances, it was perhaps her intellect and pursuit of knowledge that truly defined her reign and set her apart as one of history's most dynamic leaders. This chapter explores Cleopatra's devotion to education and learning, and how modern individuals can draw on her wisdom to fuel personal and professional growth.

Intellectual Foundation

Cleopatra's education was nothing short of comprehensive. Fluent in several languages and educated by the most learned scholars of her time, she was the only member of her dynasty to speak the

Egyptian language alongside Greek, which made her particularly beloved by her people. Her education spanned mathematics, astronomy, philosophy, and the arts, making her a true polymath in a world dominated by male scholars and rulers.

For the modern reader, Cleopatra's dedication to learning serves as a powerful reminder of the value of a broad and deep education. In today's rapidly changing world, the ability to adapt and learn new skills is invaluable. Just as Cleopatra learned the languages and customs of her people to better connect and rule, so too must today's leaders and thinkers remain perpetual students of their crafts and societies.

Cleopatra's Library

Imagine the legendary Library of Alexandria, a wonder of the ancient world, and a repository of knowledge that attracted scholars from across the Mediterranean. As a patron of this center of learning, Cleopatra ensured that she had access to the best minds and ideas of her time. The library was not just a collection of scrolls; it was a vibrant hub of intellectual activity where ideas were exchanged and knowledge expanded.

In this digital age, the entire sum of human knowledge is often just a click away. Emulating Cleopatra, modern individuals should build their own "libraries"—curating information, fostering communities of learning, and maintaining a healthy intellectual curiosity. This might involve engaging with online courses, participating in webinars, or simply dedicating time each day to read and research.

Philosophy and Governance

Cleopatra's governance was heavily influenced by her philosophical studies, particularly by the works of Plato and other Greek philosophers. She embraced the idea of the "philosopher king," a ruler who governs wisely and justly, informed by philosophy. This perspective was evident in her strategic alliances and political maneuvers, which were not just about power, but about creating stability and prosperity for her people.

For contemporary readers, integrating philosophy into daily decision-making can enhance both personal integrity and professional effectiveness. By studying philosophy, one can develop critical thinking skills, ethical reasoning, and a deeper understanding of human behavior—all crucial for navigating today's complex societal landscapes.

Steward of Culture

Cleopatra also understood the power of cultural knowledge. She famously dressed as the goddess Isis during significant public appearances, connecting herself to Egyptian spirituality and tradition in a way that resonated deeply with her subjects. Her ability to blend cultural elements into her leadership style was a testament to her deep understanding of the diverse cultures over which she ruled.

Today, cultural intelligence is increasingly recognized as a vital skill, especially in diverse, globalized environments. Understanding and appreciating cultural differences can lead to more effective communication, better conflict resolution, and more inclusive communities and workplaces.

Meditation: Mindful Learning

Let's engage in a meditation inspired by Cleopatra's pursuit of knowledge. Find a quiet space where you can sit comfortably without interruptions.

Begin by focusing on your breath. Inhale deeply and exhale slowly, allowing your mind to clear and your body to relax.

Visualize yourself in the Library of Alexandria. See the high columns and endless shelves of scrolls. Feel the cool marble under your feet and the quiet buzz of scholarly activity around you.

Approach a scroll that catches your eye. Visualize yourself unrolling it and discovering knowledge that is personally or professionally relevant to you.

Reflect on how this knowledge could impact your life. Imagine applying this wisdom in your daily interactions, your career, or your personal aspirations.

As you conclude, slowly bring your awareness back to the present. Take a deep breath and commit to a step you can take today to expand your knowledge or understanding in a specific area.

Embracing Lifelong Learning

Cleopatra's life teaches us that knowledge is not just about power; it is about connecting with others, governing wisely, and living fully. Her legacy as a learner and leader offers timeless lessons for anyone seeking to enhance their intellectual capacity and embrace the endless journey of personal growth.

As we close this chapter, let us take forward the essence of Cleopatra's intellectual spirit—curiosity, dedication, and an unwavering commitment to learning and self-improvement. These traits are just as relevant today as they were over two millennia ago in the bustling streets and grand palaces of Alexandria.

Chapter 6: Wellness Practices from Egypt

The allure of ancient Egypt extends far beyond its monumental architecture and intriguing pharaohs. Among the sands and stones, the Egyptians developed a sophisticated understanding of health and wellness, integrating natural remedies, body practices, and spiritual insights into a holistic approach to well-being. This chapter delves into the wellness practices that may have been used by Cleopatra herself and explores how these can be adapted to our modern lives.

Ancient Foundations of Health

Cleopatra VII, the last active ruler of the Ptolemaic Kingdom of Egypt, was renowned not only for her political acumen but also for her profound interest in health and beauty. The Egyptians, during her time and before, believed health was the balance between physical, mental, and spiritual elements. They were pioneers in the development of medicine, with herbalism playing a significant role in their therapeutic practices.

Herbs such as cumin, anise, mustard, and coriander were not just culinary additives but were considered potent remedies for a variety of ailments. The Egyptians used honey for its antibacterial properties, garlic for its immune-boosting effects, and aloe vera for its soothing and healing abilities on the skin.

Cleopatra's Regimen

As a queen, Cleopatra would have had access to the best health practices of her time. It's documented that she bathed in donkey milk, which was believed to preserve the youthfulness of the skin, thanks to its lactose enzymes and natural moisturizing properties. Today, the lactic acid in milk is still used as a skin-softening agent and a natural exfoliant in the beauty industry.

Cleopatra's interest in wellness likely extended beyond beauty treatments; it encompassed a holistic approach that included diet, physical exercise, and mental health practices. The Mediterranean diet, rich in grains, fruits, vegetables, and olive oil, was prevalent during her reign and remains one of the most recommended diets for health and longevity.

Movement and Physical Health

The Egyptians recognized the importance of physical activity. From the laborers who built the pyramids to the dances performed in religious ceremonies, movement was an integral part of their daily lives. Cleopatra herself is said to have practiced a form of yoga, which involved meditation and physical postures designed to enhance body flexibility and strength.

In today's world, incorporating routine physical exercise can mirror the activities of ancient Egyptians. Practices like yoga, Pilates, and Tai Chi not only promote physical health but also improve mental well-being, echoing the holistic health views of Cleopatra's time.

Spiritual and Mental Wellness

Spirituality was deeply woven into the fabric of Egyptian society. The Egyptians practiced daily rituals and prayers to communicate with the gods and seek their protection and guidance. Meditation and prayer were vital for maintaining spiritual and mental health, helping individuals find balance and peace in their lives.

Modern meditation draws on similar principles, focusing on the cultivation of inner peace, resilience, and mental clarity. By setting aside time for meditation, much like the ancient Egyptians, we can foster a greater sense of well-being and reduce stress in our lives.

Herbal Remedies and Modern Adaptations

Today, many of us are turning back to natural remedies, reflecting a resurgence of interest in the wisdom of ancient cultures like Egypt. Incorporating herbs into our daily routine can be as simple as using peppermint to aid digestion, chamomile to improve sleep, or turmeric for its anti-inflammatory properties. These practices reflect a continuity of knowledge from Cleopatra's era to our own.

Creating a modern-day herbal garden or using essential oils can be a direct way to connect with the ancient Egyptian approach to health, drawing on the natural environment as a source of healing.

Body Scans and Egyptian Healing

One of the meditation techniques that can be directly inspired by ancient Egyptian practices is the body scan. This involves mentally scanning your body for areas of tension and consciously relaxing them, a method that promotes self-awareness and healing.

Imagine lying on the warm sands of the Nile delta under the vast, starry sky. Start at the tips of your toes, gradually moving up through your limbs, torso, and head, noting any discomfort or stiffness and gently releasing it. This practice not only aids in relaxation but also aligns with the ancient Egyptian reverence for the body as a vessel that connects the physical and the divine.

Cleopatra's Egypt offers a treasure trove of insights into health and wellness, many of which are still relevant today. By exploring and adapting these ancient practices, we can tap into a wellspring of ancient wisdom that promotes a balanced, healthy lifestyle. As we integrate these old-world practices with modern science, we continue the legacy of wellness that has been handed down through the ages, proving that sometimes, looking back is the best way to move forward.

In the next chapter, we will explore how Cleopatra used her charisma to captivate not only her contemporaries but also generations to come, providing lessons on how personal magnetism can be cultivated and wielded effectively in our own lives.

Chapter 7: Cleopatra's Charisma: Harnessing the Charm of the Last Pharaoh of Egypt

Cleopatra VII, the last active ruler of the Ptolemaic Kingdom of Egypt, remains one of history's most enduring figures, not only for her political acumen but for her extraordinary charisma. Her ability to influence those around her was so profound that it altered the course of history. In this chapter, we will explore the essence of Cleopatra's charisma, dissect its components, and provide practical exercises through meditation to help you cultivate your own charismatic presence.

Understanding Charisma

Charisma is often seen as an elusive trait, something inherent that a person either possesses or does not. However, charisma can be broken down into a set of skills and qualities that can be developed and refined. At its core, charisma is about the ability to attract, charm, and influence people. For Cleopatra, this meant the ability to connect with individuals from different backgrounds and to command respect across cultural and political boundaries.

Components of Cleopatra's Charisma

Confidence: Confidence is fundamental to charisma. Cleopatra's confidence was rooted in her education, her royal status, and her self-belief. She was knowledgeable in many areas, including politics, science, and languages, which gave her the confidence to engage with powerful figures such as Julius Caesar and Mark Antony on equal footing.

Empathy: Cleopatra was known for her ability to relate to others emotionally. Her empathy wasn't just a personal trait but a strategic tool that allowed her to understand and influence the feelings and motivations of others.

Communication: A master of several languages, Cleopatra could communicate effectively with ambassadors from various parts of the world. Her skills in rhetoric and her ability to tailor her language to her audience were key aspects of her charm.

Mystique: Cleopatra cultivated an aura of mystery that made her an intriguing figure. This mystique was a combination of her exotic appearance, her intellectual depth, and her strategic self-presentation, which kept her counterparts fascinated and slightly off balance.

Practical Lessons from Cleopatra's Charisma

Cultivate Knowledge and Confidence: Invest time in learning and personal development. Broad knowledge and expertise can enhance your self-confidence and the way others perceive you.

Develop Empathy: Try to understand the emotions and motivations of those around you. This understanding can improve your interpersonal interactions and increase your influence.

Enhance Your Communication Skills: Like Cleopatra, work on your ability to communicate clearly and persuasively in multiple settings. Tailoring your message to your audience can significantly increase its impact.

Maintain a Sense of Mystique: While transparency is valuable, maintaining a certain level of mystique can make you more compelling. Share selectively and let your actions often speak for you.

Charisma-Enhancing Meditation: Visualizing Cleopatra

Now, let's engage in a meditation designed to help you embody Cleopatra's charismatic qualities. Find a quiet place where you can sit comfortably and close your eyes.

Begin by taking deep breaths: Inhale slowly through your nose, hold for a few seconds, and exhale through your mouth. Repeat this breathing exercise three times to center yourself and clear your mind.

Visualize a meeting with Cleopatra: Imagine yourself walking through the grand halls of Cleopatra's palace. The walls are adorned with exquisite hieroglyphics and golden decorations. Feel the cool marble under your feet as you walk confidently toward the throne room.

Meeting Cleopatra: See Cleopatra seated on her throne, her demeanor calm and welcoming. Notice her confident posture and the intelligent look in her eyes. As you approach, she smiles, inviting you to sit beside her.

Engage in conversation: Cleopatra begins to speak with you in a language you understand perfectly. Listen to the tone of her voice, the clarity of her words, and the persuasive grace with which she constructs her sentences. She listens intently to you, nodding in understanding.

Absorb her qualities: As you converse, imagine a gentle light emanating from Cleopatra and moving towards you. This light carries her charisma—her confidence, empathy, eloquence, and mystique. Feel these qualities entering your being, filling you with the same charismatic power.

Ending the meditation: Gradually, bring your focus back to your breathing. Feel the ground beneath you and slowly open your eyes, carrying Cleopatra's charismatic essence within you.

Repeat this meditation regularly to help internalize and cultivate the elements of charisma that made Cleopatra a figure of enduring fascination and power.

Cleopatra's charisma was a blend of her self-assurance, empathetic connection, articulate communication, and an intriguing aura. By understanding and practicing these elements, you too can develop a charismatic presence that influences and inspires those around you. Remember, charisma is not just an inborn trait but a skill set that you can enhance through conscious effort and reflection. Embrace these practices, and step into your power, just as Cleopatra once did along the banks of the Nile.

Chapter 8: Mastering Languages of Power

Cleopatra VII, the last active ruler of the Ptolemaic Kingdom of Egypt, is renowned not only for her political acumen but also for her linguistic abilities. She was a polyglot, reputed to have spoken as many as nine languages. This capability was not just a personal skill; it was a strategic tool that enabled her to communicate directly with many of her subjects and foreign dignitaries, enhancing her effectiveness as a ruler. In this chapter, we will explore how the mastery of languages served as a power tool for Cleopatra and how modern individuals can apply these lessons to increase their influence and deepen their personal and professional relationships.

The Power of Language in Leadership

Language is more than just a means of communication; it is a conduit of culture, emotions, and influence. For Cleopatra, being able to speak multiple languages meant she could negotiate, charm, and align with powerful counterparts without the barrier of an interpreter. This direct communication was key to her success in forming military and romantic alliances that sustained her reign.

In today's globalized world, the ability to communicate in multiple languages can open doors to international opportunities, foster understanding, and build trust across cultures. Leaders who invest in learning other languages demonstrate respect and empathy towards other cultures, which can translate into stronger, more effective partnerships.

Learning Languages Today

While not everyone can master nine languages, learning even one new language can have profound impacts on your cognitive abilities, including problem-solving, multitasking, and memory. The process of learning a language involves understanding the nuances that make each culture unique, which is essential for anyone looking to broaden their worldview and enhance their career in an increasingly interconnected world.

Techniques for Language Mastery

Immersive Learning: Just as Cleopatra would have learned languages through direct engagement with speakers, language learners today can benefit from immersive experiences. This could be as simple as participating in language meet-ups or as involved as traveling to a country where the language is spoken.

Utilizing Modern Technology: Leveraging apps and online courses can provide interactive and convenient ways to learn languages at your own pace. Technologies like virtual reality are also beginning to simulate immersive language learning environments without leaving your home.

Consistent Practice: Regular practice is key in language acquisition. Set daily or weekly goals to practice speaking, listening, reading, and writing. Consistency turns occasional learning into a habit and eventually into fluency.

Cultural Integration: Understanding the culture behind a language can enhance learning. Engage with films, music, and literature from the countries where the language is spoken. This cultural context can make the language come alive and enhance retention.

Applying Language Skills Strategically

The strategic use of language extends beyond mere translation. It involves understanding the emotional and cultural connotations of words and phrases in different languages. Cleopatra used her linguistic skills to appeal to the emotional and political sensibilities of her subjects and allies. Similarly, leaders today can use their language skills to navigate international negotiations, manage multinational teams, and market products across borders with sensitivity and precision.

Language as a Tool for Personal Development

Learning a language also offers significant personal benefits. It can improve cognitive flexibility, delay the onset of dementia, and increase tolerance and openness. These benefits contribute to a more adaptable and resilient mindset—qualities that are invaluable in both personal and professional spheres.

Meditation: Language Learning Visualization

To conclude this chapter, let us engage in a meditation designed to enhance your language learning journey. Find a quiet space where you can sit comfortably without interruptions. Close your eyes and take a few deep breaths to center yourself.

Imagine yourself in a bustling market in a city where your target language is spoken. Visualize the vibrant stalls, the people, and the sounds around you. You are comfortable and confident as you move through the crowd.

Approach a vendor and initiate a conversation. Imagine yourself fluently asking questions about their products, discussing prices, and even making a few jokes.

Visualize the vendor responding warmly, appreciating your effort to speak their language. Feel the connection being built as you communicate confidently.

Now, let this scene fade away as you bring your focus back to your breathing. Take a deep breath in, acknowledging the power of languages to connect and empower. Slowly open your eyes, carrying with you the confidence and readiness to tackle your language learning goals.

Cleopatra's use of languages as a tool for power and influence is a compelling reminder of the relevance of linguistic skills in any era. By embracing language learning, we open ourselves up to a multitude of opportunities for leadership, influence, and personal growth, just as Cleopatra once did.

Chapter 9: The Spiritual Practices of Cleopatra

In the pantheon of historical figures whose lives have transcended time, Cleopatra stands as a beacon of spiritual complexity and religious dedication. This chapter delves into the lesser-explored spiritual dimension of Cleopatra's reign, examining how her devout practices and religious undertakings influenced both her personal life and her rule over Egypt.

The Intersection of Religion and Politics

Cleopatra VII, the last active ruler of the Ptolemaic Kingdom of Egypt, was not only a political and strategic powerhouse but also a religious figurehead. Her reign is often remembered for its dramatic political and romantic entanglements, yet her spiritual role was equally significant. She was deemed the living embodiment of the goddess Isis, a role that was part strategic and part devout worship. This divine status was not merely symbolic; it was a central tenet of her authority, used to legitimize her reign in the eyes of her subjects.

The integration of deity status into Cleopatra's rule illustrates the intricate relationship between leadership and divine right in ancient Egypt. By aligning herself with Isis, who was associated with fertility, motherhood, and the protection of the nation, Cleopatra was able to strengthen her political position and create a personal connection with her people. This spiritual strategy was pivotal in maintaining her power and influence.

Embracing the Role of Isis

Cleopatra's identification with Isis was a multifaceted endeavor that encompassed public ceremonies, temple patronages, and her portrayal in art and coinage. Her public appearances were often staged to emphasize her divine status; she adorned herself in the traditional garb of Isis, complete with a throne and ceremonial regalia, during significant religious festivals. This public worship not only reinforced her status as a living goddess but also worked to unify her subjects under a shared religious and cultural identity.

To better understand the profound nature of Cleopatra's spiritual practice, one must consider the broader context of Egyptian religion. The people of Egypt were deeply religious, and the pharaoh's role as the intermediary between the gods and the world of humans was a cornerstone of Egyptian society. Cleopatra's active engagement in her role as Isis was not only a political maneuver but also a deeply ingrained duty that she performed with earnest devotion.

Spiritual Practices and Ceremonies

Cleopatra's reign was marked by numerous religious initiatives, including the restoration and construction of many temples dedicated to various deities. These projects served both as acts of piety and as visible symbols of her devotion and capability as a ruler. The temple of Hathor at Dendera, for instance, features inscriptions and reliefs that depict Cleopatra and her son Caesarion, co-ruling as gods in their own right, making offerings to Hathor and other deities.

Her involvement in religious festivals was another aspect of her spiritual life. These festivals not only served as public affirmations of her divine status but also as opportunities for Cleopatra to engage directly with her people, strengthening communal ties and reinforcing social and religious norms.

Meditation: A Spiritual Cleansing Meditation in the Setting of an Egyptian Temple

Let us engage in a meditation inspired by the spiritual practices of Cleopatra. Find a quiet place to sit comfortably, close your eyes, and take a deep breath. Imagine yourself walking towards a grand temple on the banks of the Nile at sunset. The sky is painted with hues of deep orange and purple, and the air is filled with the gentle scent of incense.

As you enter the temple, you see a figure in the distance, adorned in the traditional dress of Isis. It is Cleopatra, performing a ritual of purification. Join her by the sacred pool in the center of the temple. As Cleopatra recites ancient prayers, dip your hands into the water. Feel the cool liquid against your skin, cleansing you of your worldly concerns and filling you with peace.

With each word that Cleopatra chants, feel a deeper connection to the world around you. The walls of the temple are adorned with carvings of gods and goddesses, each telling stories of faith, resilience, and power. Absorb the sacred energy of this place, letting it heal and empower you.

As the ritual comes to an end, Cleopatra turns to you with a knowing smile, acknowledging your shared experience in this sacred space. You feel a profound sense of peace and empowerment, ready to bring the wisdom of the ancients into your modern life.

Slowly bring your awareness back to the present. Take a deep breath, open your eyes, and carry with you the tranquility and strength you have gained from this spiritual journey.

Cleopatra's life is a testament to the power of integrating spiritual practices into daily leadership and governance. Her role as Isis was not just a title but a deeply ingrained part of her identity and rule. This chapter has explored how her spiritual endeavors were not only personal acts of devotion but also key elements of her political strategy, showing that leadership can be profoundly enhanced by spiritual depth and authenticity. In our modern lives, we too can draw on spiritual traditions to foster a deeper connection to our communities and ourselves, embracing the wisdom of the past to inform our present.

Chapter 10: The Love Affairs That Shaped History

Cleopatra VII Philopator, the last active ruler of the Ptolemaic Kingdom of Egypt, is often remembered not only for her political acumen but also for her storied love affairs with two of the most powerful men of her time—Julius Caesar and Mark Antony. These relationships were not merely romantic entanglements but strategic alliances that shaped the political landscape of the ancient world. This chapter delves into the lessons modern readers can extract about love, power, and personal relationships from Cleopatra's liaisons, supplemented by a meditation aimed at opening the heart to love and forgiveness.

Cleopatra and Julius Caesar: A Strategic Alliance

Cleopatra's relationship with Julius Caesar began in 48 BCE, when she was smuggled into the palace rolled in a carpet—a scene emblematic of both her resourcefulness and her flair for dramatic gestures. She sought Caesar's support to reclaim her throne, which had been usurped by her brother. Caesar, captivated not only by her beauty but also by her intellect and charm, supported her cause, leading to her reinstatement as co-ruler with her younger brother.

From this relationship, we learn the importance of vision and mutual benefit in partnerships. Cleopatra and Caesar were both ambitious leaders who looked beyond mere romantic involvement; they saw a partnership that could mutually enhance their power and influence. This teaches us that at the core of a lasting relationship is not just personal affection but a shared vision for the future.

Meditation Focus: Imagine yourself walking alongside Caesar in the lush gardens of a reconstructed Alexandria, discussing future plans with clarity and mutual respect. Feel the strength of a partnership that transcends personal benefit and leans towards a shared future.

Cleopatra and Mark Antony: A Bond of Passion and Tragedy

After Caesar's assassination in 44 BCE, Cleopatra aligned herself with Mark Antony, who, like Caesar, found himself enchanted by the queen's combination of beauty, intelligence, and political savvy. Their affair was marked by both profound passion and significant political maneuvers, including the infamous Donations of Alexandria, where Antony declared Cleopatra and her children rulers over various Roman territories.

This relationship underscores the power of personal charisma and emotional connection in strengthening bonds. However, it also serves as a cautionary tale about the risks of allowing passion to overshadow practical considerations. Antony's alliance with Cleopatra ultimately led to his downfall and suicide, and Cleopatra's subsequent demise marked the end of the Ptolemaic Kingdom.

Meditation Focus: Visualize a sunset boat ride on the Nile with Antony, the air filled with the promise of undying love and the peril of great risk. Reflect on balancing deep emotional connections with the practicalities that ground them.

Lessons in Love and Power

Cleopatra's relationships provide profound insights into the complex interplay between love and power. First, they show that relationships can be strategic as well as personal, serving broader goals beyond the individuals involved. They also highlight the importance of maintaining a balance between passion and pragmatism.

In personal relationships, as in politics, every alliance has potential benefits and risks. Cleopatra's liaisons remind us of the need for clear communication, shared goals, and mutual respect. They also caution against the potential for relationships to blind individuals to other obligations and realities.

Meditation Focus: Engage in a heart-opening meditation. Imagine your heart expanding with each breath, enveloping you in warmth and light. With each exhale, release any bitterness or regret, making space for love and forgiveness. Envision yourself in Cleopatra's royal chamber, making decisions that balance heart and mind.

Embracing Modern Relationships with Ancient Wisdom

Today, we can draw on Cleopatra's experiences to enhance our personal and professional relationships. Understanding the dynamics of her partnerships with Caesar and Antony can help us navigate our own relationships with greater awareness and strategy. Whether seeking a partner to co-navigate the complexities of life or building professional alliances, the principles of mutual benefit, shared vision, emotional intelligence, and balance remain relevant.

As we conclude this chapter, consider how the essence of Cleopatra's relationships can inform your approach to modern love and partnerships. Let her life remind you that while love can indeed shape history, it must be nurtured with wisdom, balance, and foresight.

Final Meditation Focus: Sit in quiet reflection, considering the relationships in your life. Are they balanced? Do they serve mutual purposes? Allow Cleopatra's legacy to guide you in cultivating relationships that are not only fulfilling but also empowering. As you meditate, envision your relationships flourishing under the principles of shared growth, respect, and profound connection.

Chapter 11: Fashion and Adornment: Exploring the Symbolism and Power of Royal Attire in Cleopatra's Egypt

Fashion in ancient Egypt was not merely about aesthetics; it was a complex language of power, identity, and divine connection. This chapter delves into the intricate world of fashion and adornment during Cleopatra's reign, exploring how her strategic use of clothing and jewelry not only enhanced her allure but also cemented her status as a political and spiritual figurehead.

The Role of Fashion in Cleopatra's Reign

Cleopatra VII, the last active ruler of the Ptolemaic Kingdom of Egypt, understood the power of visual representation. She was not only a queen but also a shrewd politician who utilized every tool at her disposal to communicate her authority and divine right to rule. Fashion was one of these tools. Cleopatra's clothing choices were never arbitrary; they were meticulously planned to convey specific messages to her audience, whether they were her subjects, political allies, or rivals.

Her wardrobe was a blend of Egyptian and Hellenistic elements, reflecting her dual heritage and political acumen. She often appeared in public dressed in traditional Egyptian attire, complete with the vulture headdress, to emphasize her role as the living embodiment of the goddess Isis. This not only reinforced her position in the eyes of her Egyptian subjects but also showcased her as a deity in her own right, a strategic move to maintain loyalty and control.

Symbolism in Jewelry and Adornments

Cleopatra's jewelry was laden with symbols. Each piece she wore carried cultural or religious significance, crafted to enhance her divine status among the Egyptians and to project power and wealth. For example, the use of lapis lazuli, a deep blue stone, in her necklaces was significant. The stone was associated with the heavens in ancient Egyptian mythology, suggesting a divine favor.

Her famous pearl earrings, as recounted in the story of her banquet with Marc Antony, were not just displays of immense wealth but also a symbol of her command over the riches of the East. Pearls, rare and valuable, represented the wealth of the oceans and Cleopatra's control over the Mediterranean trade routes.

The Impact of Royal Attire on Diplomacy

Cleopatra's fashion also played a crucial role in her diplomatic endeavors. Her well-documented encounter with Julius Caesar, where she allegedly unrolled herself from a woven carpet, showcases her understanding of drama and attire. It is said that she wore a gown that emphasized her royal status and allure, which not only captivated Caesar but also positioned her as a formidable ally rather than a supplicant.

Similarly, during her famous trips to Rome, Cleopatra's choice of attire was designed to impress and intimidate the Roman populace and elite. Her exotic, luxurious clothing, imbued with symbolism from her homeland, served to make her stand out in the Roman political theater, crafting an image of a powerful foreign queen not to be underestimated.

Fashion as a Tool for Personal and Political Narratives

Cleopatra's use of fashion went beyond personal vanity. It was a calculated component of her political strategy. By dressing in styles that evoked the imagery of gods and goddesses, she was not just adopting divine attributes; she was telling a story of herself that transcended the human realm. This narrative was powerful in a deeply religious society where the divine right of kings – or in Cleopatra's case, queens - was uncontested.

In public appearances and state functions, her attire was always chosen to reflect the occasion's specific needs. Whether it was a military review where she presented herself as a commander, or a religious ceremony where she appeared as a high priestess, her fashion choices reinforced her multifaceted role as ruler, deity, and military leader.

Cleopatra's Legacy in Fashion

The legacy of Cleopatra's fashion sense continues to inspire even today. Modern interpretations of her style emphasize luxury and boldness, traits that have been immortalized in film and popular culture. However, the real lesson from Cleopatra's use of fashion is deeper and more nuanced. It is about the power of clothing and adornment to craft one's identity, convey messages, and execute power dynamics without uttering a single word.

Meditation: Visualizing Royal Attire

Now, let us engage in a meditation that connects us with the power of Cleopatra's fashion. Close your eyes and imagine yourself in the heart of ancient Egypt. Visualize walking into a room adorned with the riches of the Nile. Feel a robe of finest linen draped around your shoulders, heavy with golden embroidery that catches the light with every movement.

See yourself approaching a mirror, and with each step, adorn yourself with jewelry that bears significant symbols—each piece a testament to your authority and divine protection. With every item you wear, feel your stature rising, your presence filling the room.

This meditation is not about vanity. It is about understanding the power of symbols and how they can be used to project our inner strength and intentions. Just as Cleopatra used her attire to communicate her capabilities and intentions, you can harness the power of your personal presentation to shape how you are perceived and how you influence the world around you.

Through this journey into Cleopatra's world of fashion and adornment, we find that our exterior can reflect our deepest intentions and potentials, acting as a bridge between our inner world and how we engage with the outer world.

Chapter 12: Cleopatra's Influence on Roman Politics

Cleopatra VII, the last active ruler of the Ptolemaic Kingdom of Egypt, remains a figure shrouded in both mystique and historical significance. Her intelligence, political savvy, and undeniable charm not only secured her place on the throne of Egypt but also allowed her to significantly influence Roman politics during her reign. This chapter explores how Cleopatra adeptly maneuvered through the complex web of Roman power structures to maintain her kingdom's sovereignty and how modern leaders can draw lessons from her strategies.

Cleopatra's Entry into Roman Affairs

Cleopatra's involvement with Rome began in earnest when she aligned herself with Julius Caesar, a connection that would prove to be the first of several alliances with powerful Roman figures. Her liaison with Caesar was not merely romantic; it was a calculated political move designed to strengthen her position in Egypt and on the international stage. By aligning with Caesar, Cleopatra gained a powerful ally in Rome, securing military backing that would help her reclaim the throne from her brother and co-ruler, Ptolemy XIII.

Leveraging Personal Relationships

The alliance with Caesar exemplifies Cleopatra's skill in using personal relationships to achieve political goals. Her ability to forge and maintain these relationships was pivotal. After Caesar's assassination, Cleopatra aligned with Mark Antony, another prominent Roman politician and military leader. With Antony, her strategy was similar: create a personal bond that translates into political allegiance. Their relationship was mutually beneficial, as Antony needed both the material and military resources that Egypt could provide.

Diplomatic Brilliance

Cleopatra's influence in Roman politics was also evident in her diplomatic engagements. She was a master of public relations and used her image strategically to assert her power and legitimacy. When she met Antony in Tarsus, she famously arrived on a barge adorned with the trappings of a goddess, presenting herself not merely as a queen but as a divine figure. This theatrical entrance was designed to impress and sway Antony, showcasing her understanding of the power of spectacle in diplomacy.

Strategic Use of Resources

Cleopatra understood the importance of Egypt's economic resources in her political maneuverings. Egypt was the breadbasket of the Mediterranean, and by controlling the grain supply, Cleopatra held a significant lever over Rome, which depended heavily on Egyptian grain. Her ability to manipulate this dependency ensured that Rome had a vested interest in her stability and success. Cleopatra's strategic control over these resources highlights her acumen in using economic tools to bolster her political objectives.

Influence through Patronage

Cleopatra also extended her influence through patronage. She supported the arts, literature, and education, projecting the image of a cultured and enlightened monarch. This patronage was not only for the benefit of her own people but also served as a soft power strategy, enhancing her standing among the Roman elite who valued cultural sophistication. Through these contributions, she intertwined her image with the ideals of intellectual and artistic excellence, further solidifying her influence in Roman circles.

Navigating Political Turbulence

Cleopatra's political journey was not without its challenges. Her involvement in Roman affairs came at a time of significant upheaval in Rome, with power struggles and civil war shaping the political landscape. Cleopatra's ability to navigate this turbulence was a testament to her political foresight and adaptability. She remained flexible, aligning with the prevailing powers when necessary and always keeping the interests of Egypt at the forefront of her strategies.

Legacy and Lessons

Cleopatra's influence on Roman politics extends beyond her lifetime. She left a legacy of a leader who could adeptly navigate and manipulate the structures of power to her advantage. Modern leaders can learn from her ability to use diplomatic channels effectively, manage resources strategically, and maintain personal relationships that align with broader political objectives.

Meditative Reflection: Visualizing Influence

Let us engage in a meditation to harness the wisdom of Cleopatra in our own endeavors. Imagine yourself walking through the bustling streets of ancient Rome, aware of the intricate web of alliances and power structures that define the city. As you walk, visualize yourself meeting influential figures, engaging them with charm and intelligence as Cleopatra might have. Feel the confidence she possessed, knowing the strength of her resources and the allure of her personality.

This meditative journey encourages us to reflect on our own resources and relationships. Consider how you can utilize your personal strengths and strategic assets to influence and lead effectively in your own sphere, drawing inspiration from Cleopatra's remarkable legacy.

Cleopatra's story teaches us that the art of influence is perennial, transcending time and geography. Her strategies in Roman politics—leveraging personal relationships, managing resources, and employing diplomacy—offer timeless lessons for anyone who seeks to wield influence wisely and effectively.

Chapter 13: The Mother of a Dynasty

Cleopatra VII, the last active ruler of the Ptolemaic Kingdom of Egypt, was not only a political and cultural icon but also a devoted mother. Her role as a progenitor of a dynasty offers profound lessons on nurturing, strategic planning, and legacy building. This chapter explores how the values and strategies Cleopatra employed in her motherhood can inspire modern parents and leaders aiming to leave a lasting impact on their own legacies.

The Maternal Role of Cleopatra

Cleopatra's motherhood is often overshadowed by her political maneuvers and romantic liaisons, yet her role as a mother was central to her agenda of securing her family's rule. She was a mother to Caesarion, her son with Julius Caesar, and three other children with Mark Antony: Alexander Helios, Cleopatra Selene, and Ptolemy Philadelphus. Each child was not just a beloved offspring but a key piece in Cleopatra's broader political strategy. She sought to carve out a future for her children that would extend the influence of the Ptolemaic dynasty far beyond Egypt's borders.

Strategic Nurturing

Cleopatra was acutely aware of the environments her children grew up in. She aimed to provide not only love and care but also education and preparation for their future roles as leaders. This strategic nurturing involved imparting wisdom, teaching leadership skills, and instilling a strong sense of duty and awareness of their heritage.

In the same vein, modern parenting can take cues from Cleopatra by being purposeful in how we raise future generations. This involves more than providing for children's basic needs and extends to equipping them with the skills and values needed to navigate and improve the world. Parents and leaders today can foster environments that encourage curiosity, resilience, and ethical leadership, preparing children to tackle the challenges of their own eras.

Building Alliances Through Maternity

Cleopatra understood the power of alliances. Each of her children was a potential link to strengthening relationships with powerful external entities. For example, her son Caesarion was not merely the child of a Roman and an Egyptian but a living symbol of the alliance between the two great powers of the age. Similarly, the birth of her children with Mark Antony solidified her personal and political bonds with Rome.

Today's leaders can learn from Cleopatra's approach by recognizing the power of partnerships and collaborative efforts in both business and personal spheres. Building strong relationships can be pivotal in achieving long-term success and stability. In modern terms, this could translate into forming strategic partnerships that align with one's long-term goals and values.

The Challenge of Legacy

For Cleopatra, ensuring that her children could inherit and sustain her legacy was paramount. She was not merely raising heirs; she was molding future rulers. This aspect of her motherhood was intertwined with her vision for Egypt's future, reflecting her commitment to both her country and her family.

In reflecting on our own lives, the concept of legacy extends beyond biological offspring. It encompasses the impact we have on our communities and the professional and personal legacies we leave behind. By embracing Cleopatra's long-term vision, individuals today can focus on creating sustainable impacts that transcend their immediate presence and continue to influence positively.

A Legacy of Wisdom

Cleopatra's efforts as a mother were ultimately geared towards instilling wisdom and a regal bearing in her children. She wanted them to not only inherit a kingdom but to rule it with intelligence, compassion, and strength. Her approach to parenting underscores the importance of educating children not just in academic subjects but in life skills and moral values.

Parents today can take this aspect of Cleopatra's legacy to heart by prioritizing holistic education that prepares children for all facets of life, not just the professional sphere. Teaching children about cultural awareness, ethical decision-making, and social responsibility are just as crucial as traditional schooling.

Meditation: Nurturing Future Generations

Let us engage in a meditation that focuses on nurturing and legacy. Find a quiet space and take a few deep breaths to center yourself.

Imagine you are in the lush gardens of Alexandria. The air is filled with the scent of the sea and blooming flowers. Before you is a young sapling, representing the future generation. As you water this sapling, envision each droplet as a lesson or value you wish to pass on. With each nurturing act, see the tree grow stronger and taller, its branches reaching out wide into the sky.

Reflect on the legacy you wish to cultivate. What values do you want to instill in this growing tree? How can you ensure it thrives and stands resilient against the winds of change? Take a few moments to imagine the tree fully grown, sheltering and inspiring those who seek its shade.

Cleopatra's role as a mother was as strategic and impactful as her role as a queen. By examining her maternal practices, modern individuals can gain insights into nurturing leadership, strategic alliance-building, and the cultivation of a lasting legacy. Like the Queen of the Nile, today's leaders and parents are tasked with preparing the ground for the next generation's success and well-being. Through strategic nurturing and thoughtful legacy-building, we can hope to leave a mark that endures through the ages.

Chapter 14: Building Alliances

In the annals of history, Cleopatra VII stands out not only for her undeniable charm and intelligence but also for her strategic acumen in forming alliances that were crucial to maintaining her power and influence. This chapter explores how Cleopatra's ability to create powerful partnerships can teach us about the importance of alliances in our personal and professional lives. By examining her tactics and the lessons they hold, we can learn to cultivate our networks with the same finesse and strategic insight.

The Art of Alliances

Cleopatra's reign was marked by her relationships with two of the most powerful men of her time: Julius Caesar and Mark Antony. These were not merely romantic liaisons but strategic alliances that positioned Egypt in a place of power between competing Roman factions.

Her initial alliance with Julius Caesar allowed her to regain the throne from her brother and co-ruler, while her later relationship with Mark Antony solidified her position and brought mutual military and economic benefits.

What Cleopatra understood well was the importance of selecting allies who could provide mutual benefits. Her choices were calculated to ensure that both sides would gain from the alliance. This principle is crucial in today's world, where successful partnerships should not be based merely on the benefit to one party but on a symbiotic relationship that enhances each participant's goals.

Cultivating Mutual Benefit

To apply Cleopatra's strategy in modern settings, one must first identify potential allies who share similar goals and have resources or capabilities that complement one's own. This requires a deep understanding of one's own strengths and weaknesses, as well as those of potential partners. Cleopatra's ability to align with Rome, the superpower of her day, demonstrated her understanding of leveraging her own resources—Egypt's wealth and grain—to meet the needs of her allies.

In professional contexts, this might look like partnering with another business to expand your market reach or combining resources to tackle larger projects than you could handle alone. In personal settings, it could involve aligning with individuals whose skills or networks can help you achieve common objectives, such as community projects or personal development goals.

Strategic Communication

Cleopatra was known for her eloquence and persuasive skills, which were vital in her negotiations. Effective communication is fundamental in forming and maintaining alliances. It involves clear articulation of what each party wants from the relationship and regular interaction to ensure alignment and address any issues.

Modern communication tools provide various platforms for maintaining dialogue, but the principles of honesty, clarity, and regularity remain the foundation of effective communication. Whether it's through regular meetings, updates, or collaborative sessions, keeping communication channels open is essential for the health of any alliance.

Navigating Challenges

Alliances, however, are not without their challenges. Cleopatra's relationships with her Roman allies were fraught with political tension and personal risk. The key to navigating such challenges lies in maintaining flexibility and adaptability—qualities that Cleopatra exemplified through her reign.

When alliances face challenges, whether from external pressures or internal disagreements, the ability to adapt and find mutually beneficial solutions becomes crucial. This might mean renegotiating terms, shifting strategies, or sometimes, disengaging from the alliance if it no longer serves its purpose.

Lessons in Loyalty

Loyalty was another cornerstone of Cleopatra's alliances. Her personal and political loyalty to Julius Caesar, even after his death, ensured her support from the Caesarian faction in Rome. Similarly, her alliance with Mark Antony was marked by mutual loyalty until their tragic end. Loyalty builds trust, and trust is the glue that holds alliances together.

In today's fast-paced world, where change is constant, the value of loyalty in partnerships can sometimes be overlooked. However, maintaining loyalty can lead to long-term benefits, building a reputation of reliability and trustworthiness.

Cultivating Alliances Today

Meditative practice can help in cultivating the qualities necessary for building successful alliances. Let's engage in a meditation focused on envisioning successful alliances:

Find a quiet place and close your eyes. Take deep, slow breaths to center yourself.

Visualize a meeting with a potential ally. Imagine a setting where both of you are discussing your goals and how you can help each other succeed.

Focus on mutual benefits. Visualize a project or goal that you are working on together, see it coming to successful completion, benefiting both parties.

Reflect on the values of communication and loyalty. Envision ongoing dialogues and the deepening of trust over time.

End with a sense of gratitude. Feel thankful for the alliances you have and those you will form in the future.

Through strategic thinking, effective communication, and a commitment to mutual benefits, we can build alliances that are as enduring and influential as those that defined Cleopatra's rule. By applying ancient wisdom to modern contexts, we can navigate the complexities of relationships and harness the power of collaborations to achieve shared successes.

Chapter 15: Resilience in the Face of Adversity

Cleopatra VII, the last pharaoh of Egypt, remains an emblem of resilience and adaptability. Her reign, marked by political turmoil and personal setbacks, showcases how one can navigate through storms with grace and tenacity. In this chapter, we explore how the essence of Cleopatra's resilience can be distilled into lessons for our own lives, accompanied by a meditation exercise designed to cultivate our inner strength.

The Foundation of Cleopatra's Resilience

Cleopatra's life was a series of intense challenges. From the loss of her father which thrust her into power, to the complexities of securing her throne amidst a male-dominated world and the Roman political influence, her journey was fraught with obstacles. Yet, she managed not only to retain her power but also to expand it, largely due to her ability to adapt to changing circumstances and her unyielding determination to protect her country and its interests.

One of the first lessons we can learn from Cleopatra is the importance of strategic flexibility. She was a master at forming alliances that bolstered her position. Her liaisons with Julius Caesar and later, Mark Antony, were not just romantic encounters but strategic moves to solidify her power and protect Egypt's interests. From these relationships, she gained political clout and military support, which were crucial in a time when her reign was continually threatened.

Facing Loss and Betrayal

Throughout her reign, Cleopatra faced immense personal and political betrayal and loss. Her relationships with Rome's most powerful leaders put her in a precarious position that led to political isolation and betrayal by those she had trusted. After the assassination of Julius Caesar, Cleopatra had to navigate the treacherous political waters to align herself with Mark Antony, which was not without its risks and eventual heartbreak.

Her resilience in the face of these betrayals teaches us the power of emotional fortitude. Cleopatra's ability to mourn her losses, reassess her position, and proceed with renewed determination is a powerful lesson in not allowing setbacks to derail our objectives.

Cultivating Resilience Through Innovation

Cleopatra also demonstrated resilience through her approach to the economic and cultural initiatives she undertook. She initiated significant architectural and cultural projects that not only beautified Alexandria but also bolstered its economy and cultural standing. This kind of innovation in times of peace and conflict illustrated her foresight and her commitment to her kingdom's prosperity and legacy.

From this, we learn the importance of continuous improvement and innovation. In our own lives, resilience can be fostered by continually seeking to improve our circumstances, regardless of the external pressures we face. By focusing on growth and development, we can maintain momentum and prevent adversity from stalling our progress.

Meditation Exercise: Building Inner Strength

To integrate Cleopatra's resilience into our lives, let us engage in a meditation focused on building inner strength. This exercise will help you visualize overcoming personal trials and emerging stronger.

Find a Quiet Space: Sit in a comfortable position in a quiet space where you won't be disturbed. Close your eyes and take several deep breaths to center yourself.

Visualize a Desert Storm: Imagine yourself in the vast, open landscapes of ancient Egypt, facing a powerful desert storm. Feel the wind and the sand against your skin. Acknowledge the challenge the storm presents, but also recognize your own strength and stability.

Stand Firm: As you face this storm, visualize yourself standing firm. With each gust of wind, feel your resilience building. You are unmovable, grounded, powerful.

Overcome the Storm: Now, visualize the storm beginning to subside. As the winds die down and the sand settles, feel a sense of triumph and calmness enveloping you. Recognize that you have the strength to withstand great forces and prevail.

Reflect on Your Resilience: As you come out of the meditation, think about the personal storms you've faced or are currently facing. Remind yourself of your strength and ability to overcome adversity, just like Cleopatra.

Slowly Return: Gently bring your awareness back to the present. Open your eyes when you're ready.

Applying Cleopatra's Lessons

Cleopatra's life teaches us that resilience is not just about surviving through adversity, but also about thriving despite it. By embracing strategic flexibility, emotional fortitude, and continuous innovation, we can cultivate a resilient spirit akin to Cleopatra's. This resilience empowers us to face our modern-day challenges with confidence and strength, ensuring that no matter what storms we encounter, we remain as enduring as the legacy of the last Queen of Egypt.

Chapter 16: The Power of Symbolism

In the annals of history, few have mastered the art of symbolism as effectively as Cleopatra VII, the last active ruler of the Ptolemaic Kingdom of Egypt. Her reign is noted not only for its political and romantic intrigues but also for the sophisticated use of symbols that communicated her power, legitimacy, and divine status to her subjects and enemies alike. This chapter delves into how symbols can convey deep messages, influence perception, and shape reality, offering insights into how modern individuals can harness this power in their personal and professional lives.

The Art of Symbolism in Cleopatra's Reign

Cleopatra's use of symbolism was a critical tool in her strategic arsenal. From the way she presented herself in public appearances to the images she chose to display on coinage, every choice was imbued with meaning designed to reinforce her position and authority. For example, Cleopatra often portrayed herself as Isis, the Egyptian goddess of health, marriage, and wisdom, thereby not only linking herself to divine powers but also securing her place in the religious and cultural heartbeats of her people.

Similarly, during her famous encounter with Julius Caesar, Cleopatra chose to be smuggled into the royal palace inside a rolled rug—a dramatic entrance that symbolized her cunning, resourcefulness, and the lengths she would go to secure her throne. This act was not only a political maneuver but a theatrical symbol that emphasized her intelligence and audacity.

Understanding Symbolism

Symbolism involves the use of symbols to represent ideas and qualities by giving them symbolic meanings that are different from their literal sense. For instance, a chain can symbolize union as well as imprisonment. In the context of Cleopatra's reign, symbolism was a powerful communicator that transcended the spoken language and reached people across the diverse empire.

The Power of Visual Symbolism

Visual symbols are incredibly potent because they can communicate complex messages quickly and effectively across different languages and cultures. Cleopatra's coinage, which often depicted her alongside divine symbols or in the guise of a goddess, served to communicate her supposed divinity and authority to those who used these coins. These images were a daily reminder of her power and divine right to govern, embedding her status in both the economy and the culture of the time.

Symbolism in Modern Contexts

Today, the use of symbolism is everywhere—from corporate logos that communicate a company's core values to personal brands that use specific colors and fonts to convey particular attributes. Understanding how to manipulate symbolism can give individuals the same edge it gave Cleopatra. For example, a professional might choose to wear glasses to a meeting to subconsciously communicate intelligence and diligence, or a company might use a lion in its branding to project strength and courage.

Crafting Your Symbolic Image

Identify Your Values: What are the core values or attributes you wish to communicate through your symbolism? Cleopatra valued intelligence, power, and divinity, and everything from her personal attire to public imagery reflected these attributes.

Choose Your Symbols Wisely: Once you know what you want to symbolize, choose symbols that best represent these qualities. If resilience is a quality you admire, symbols like the phoenix, known for rising from its ashes, could be a powerful emblem to incorporate into your personal or professional branding.

Be Consistent: Cleopatra's consistent use of certain symbols helped to solidify her image and message across Egypt and beyond. Similarly, consistency in your symbolic expressions ensures that your message is clear and memorable.

Meditative Practice: Visualizing Your Symbols

Let's engage in a meditative practice to help you visualize and connect with your personal symbols.

Step 1: Relaxation: Find a quiet space. Sit comfortably and close your eyes. Take deep, slow breaths to relax your mind and body.

Step 2: Visualization: Imagine a blank canvas before you. Slowly, let the symbols that represent your core values appear on this canvas. Visualize these symbols clearly—consider their colors, shapes, and the emotions they evoke.

Step 3: Connection: Reflect on how these symbols represent aspects of your identity. Feel the attributes they symbolize permeating your being, enhancing those qualities within you.

Step 4: Implementation: Think about how you can start incorporating these symbols into your life. Whether it's through personal attire, a logo, or even the decor of your workspace, envision how these symbols can become a part of your everyday existence.

Cleopatra's mastery of symbolism was not merely about personal vanity; it was a crucial element of her strategy to maintain power and influence. Similarly, in the modern world, understanding and using symbolism can enhance personal branding and communication. By carefully choosing and consistently using symbols that reflect your deepest values and aspirations, you can craft a persona that communicates powerfully and subtly—much like Cleopatra's did over two thousand years ago. Embrace the power of symbolism, and let it open new dimensions of influence and perception in your life.

Chapter 17: Legacy and Memory

Cleopatra VII, the last pharaoh of ancient Egypt, remains an enduring figure in history not only because of her political acumen and romantic liaisons but also due to her deliberate efforts in crafting a legacy that transcended time. In this chapter, we explore how Cleopatra consciously shaped her legacy and how we, too, can apply her wisdom to create lasting impressions in our own lives.

Crafting a Legacy

Cleopatra understood the power of legacy. Her life was a carefully orchestrated series of events designed to ensure her eternal remembrance. From monumental constructions to cultivating her image as a goddess, Cleopatra's strategies were meticulously planned. What can we learn from this? First and foremost, creating a legacy requires intention and vision.

Intentionality: Cleopatra was not passive about her legacy. She took active steps to influence how she would be remembered. This is a crucial lesson for anyone aiming to leave a mark on the world. It begins with a clear understanding of one's values and objectives. Reflect on what is truly important to you. What values do you wish to be remembered for? Integrity, kindness, innovation? Start by defining these core values, and let them guide your actions.

Vision: Cleopatra's vision was to be remembered as a powerful, divine ruler. For us, the vision might be less grandiose but equally significant. Whether it's influencing your community, excelling in your professional field, or being a great parent, your vision for your legacy should resonate deeply with your personal aspirations. Once your vision is clear, every decision you make will start to contribute towards this larger picture.

Communicating a Legacy

Cleopatra was a master communicator. Her fluency in multiple languages and her ability to engage with different cultures were pivotal. Her legacy was partly built on her reputation as a cultured and wise leader, which she communicated through her actions and the way she presented herself.

Consistency: Your legacy is built day by day, interaction by interaction. Cleopatra maintained her regal demeanor and intelligence in all her dealings. In modern times, this translates into consistency in how we present ourselves both in personal and professional settings. Your social media profiles, public interactions, and daily behaviors all contribute to the legacy you are building.

Storytelling: Cleopatra's life was a compelling story, full of drama, romance, and political intrigue. She used storytelling to her advantage, mythologizing her own life. We can use storytelling to share our experiences, lessons, and values. Sharing stories that embody our beliefs can profoundly impact others and strengthen our legacy.

Preserving a Legacy

Cleopatra's legacy was preserved through various means, including coins bearing her likeness and alliances through her children. While we may not mint coins or forge dynasties, there are modern equivalents in preserving our legacy.

Documentation: Write down your thoughts, lessons, and experiences. Whether it's through a blog, a book, or social media, documenting your journey allows you to influence others and extend your legacy beyond your immediate circle. It also serves as a reflection of your growth and values.

Mentorship: Cleopatra influenced her own legacy through her children and her political alliances.

Similarly, mentorship allows us to impart our knowledge and values to the next generation. By mentoring others, we extend our influence and ensure that our lessons and values live on.

Community Involvement: Engaging with and contributing to your community can cement your legacy. Whether through volunteer work, public service, or active participation in local organizations, being involved in community efforts ensures that you leave a tangible impact on the lives of others.

Meditation: Envisioning Your Legacy

Let's engage in a meditation to crystallize our vision of the legacy we wish to leave.

Find a quiet space where you can sit comfortably without interruptions.

Close your eyes, take a deep breath, and relax your body. With each exhale, release any tension you feel.

Visualize your future self many years from now. What achievements do you see? How are people talking about you? What impact have you made?

Reflect on the values that guided you there. What principles did you hold dear? How did these influence your decisions and actions?

Imagine the stories others tell about you. What are the lessons they have learned from you? How have you inspired or supported them?

Hold onto this vision and slowly bring yourself back to the present. Take a deep breath and open your eyes when you're ready.

Cleopatra's life teaches us that our legacy is not just what we leave for people; it's also what we leave in people. By living intentionally, communicating effectively, and preserving our values, we can ensure that our legacy endures. Like Cleopatra, let us strive not just for remembrance, but for a timeless impact that resonates through generations.

Chapter 18: The Wisdom of Ruling

Cleopatra VII, the last active ruler of the Ptolemaic Kingdom of Egypt, remains an epitome of sagacious governance and adept policy-making. Her reign, marked by astute political maneuvers and an intricate understanding of power dynamics, offers timeless lessons on leadership and governance. In this chapter, we delve into the principles of effective ruling through the lens of Cleopatra's strategies and explore how these ancient insights can inform modern leadership.

Cleopatra: A Connoisseur of Power

Cleopatra's rise to power was anything but ordinary. Born into a dynasty fraught with internal strife and external threats, she learned early on that to survive and thrive in such a volatile environment required not only raw intelligence but also exceptional political acumen. Cleopatra's ability to re-establish her rule, after being ousted by her brother, speaks volumes about her mastery in political strategy and resilience.

The first lesson from Cleopatra's rule is the importance of strategic partnerships. Her alliances with Julius Caesar and later Mark Antony were not mere romantic endeavors but calculated political moves to strengthen her position against her adversaries, both within and outside Egypt. These alliances highlight the critical role of diplomacy and relationships in governance, emphasizing that leaders must cultivate beneficial alliances to enhance their authority and secure their state's interests.

Governance Through Cultural Integration

One of Cleopatra's most notable contributions to governance was her approach to cultural integration. Unlike many conquerors who imposed their cultures on those they ruled, Cleopatra embraced Egyptian customs and religion. She was the first in her family to learn the Egyptian language and often participated in local religious practices, which endeared her to her subjects and solidified her power.

This integration teaches modern leaders the importance of respect and inclusivity. By embracing the culture of those you lead, you can foster loyalty and a sense of shared identity, which are crucial for stability and harmony within a state.

Economic Acumen

Cleopatra also demonstrated profound economic acumen. She undertook several measures to stabilize and enhance Egypt's economy. Her reign saw the revaluation of the Egyptian currency, extensive building projects, and the development of trade routes. These initiatives not only boosted Egypt's economy but also reinforced her image as a sovereign who cared for her people's welfare.

Today's leaders can learn from Cleopatra's focus on economic stability and development. A thriving economy not only improves the quality of life for the populace but also strengthens a leader's position and the country's standing on the global stage.

Cleopatra's Public Works

The infrastructure projects initiated under Cleopatra's rule were yet another aspect of her wise governance. She understood that public works not only serve economic functions but also act as a tool for public relations, showcasing the government's role in improving the lives of its citizens.

Leaders today can draw on this strategy to bolster public approval and foster a sense of community and pride among the populace. Infrastructure development remains a potent tool for economic and social enhancement.

Judicial Reforms

Cleopatra's rule also saw judicial reforms, which aimed at providing a fair and efficient system of justice. This not only helped in maintaining law and order but also in ensuring that the public viewed the governance system as just and equitable.

Modern governance can take a cue from this, understanding that a fair legal system is foundational to public trust and societal stability. It emphasizes that the rule of law is paramount and must be upheld to ensure fairness and justice for all citizens.

A Focus on Education and Scholarship

Cleopatra was known for her support of the arts and scholarship, particularly the famous Library of Alexandria. By fostering an environment where learning and culture flourished, she ensured that Egypt remained a beacon of knowledge and culture in the ancient world.

This highlights the crucial role of education and intellectual enrichment in governance. Leaders who invest in education and culture can drive innovation, inspire creativity, and enhance their nation's competitiveness.

The Modern Cleopatra

Embodying the spirit of Cleopatra in today's complex world means integrating these ancient principles of leadership into modern governance. It involves being strategic in forming alliances, embracing cultural diversity, prioritizing economic development, investing in public works, reforming judicial systems, and championing education.

Meditation: Governing a Kingdom for a Day

To conclude this chapter, engage in a guided meditation that allows you to visualize ruling a kingdom for a day.

Close your eyes and imagine yourself in a majestic palace, overlooking a vast and bustling city. Feel the weight of the crown upon your head and the responsibility it entails. Visualize walking through the city streets, observing various aspects of daily life and governance. See yourself making decisions that affect the lives of thousands—decisions that are just, that promote economic prosperity, and that foster cultural harmony.

Reflect on these responsibilities and visualize the impact of your choices on your people and their future. Let this meditation inspire you to incorporate Cleopatra's wisdom into your leadership style, aiming for a rule that is remembered for its fairness, prosperity, and benevolence.

This chapter on Cleopatra's wisdom in ruling not only highlights her enduring legacy but also serves as a guide for anyone aspiring to lead with insight, integrity, and inclusivity. By studying her life and reign, modern leaders can glean valuable lessons that are as relevant today as they were over two millennia ago.

Chapter 19: Cleopatra and the Arts: Cultivating Culture Through Patronage

Cleopatra VII, the last active ruler of the Ptolemaic Kingdom of Egypt, was not only a political and military strategist but also a renowned patron of the arts. Her reign marked a period of cultural renaissance that mirrored the sophistication and grandeur of her personality and political acumen. This chapter delves into how Cleopatra used the arts as a tool for both political influence and personal expression, and explores how we can apply these principles to enrich our own lives and environments.

The Role of Arts in Cleopatra's Reign

Cleopatra's court was a vibrant hub for intellectuals, artists, and scholars. By fostering an environment that encouraged artistic expression, she not only enhanced her image as a cultured sovereign but also strengthened her political stature through cultural diplomacy. Art in Cleopatra's time was not merely for aesthetic enjoyment but a means to communicate power, immortalize her reign, and align herself with the divine.

One of the most significant aspects of her patronage was her revival of the Pharaonic tradition, which was steeped in both symbolism and spirituality. Cleopatra portrayed herself as the reincarnation of the goddess Isis, masterfully using religious iconography to solidify her rule and divine right to govern. The statues, temples, and coins of her time were meticulously crafted to reflect this divine association, helping to reinforce her status both within Egypt and in the broader Mediterranean world.

Learning from Cleopatra's Cultural Strategies

Integration of Arts into Daily Life: Cleopatra understood that the arts could enhance daily life, making it richer and more meaningful. She surrounded herself with the finest decorations and wore elaborate clothing and jewelry that reflected Egyptian craftsmanship and luxury. This integration of beauty and art into daily routines not only improved her quality of life but also set a standard of living that was admired and emulated by her contemporaries.

Innovation Through Cultural Fusion: Despite her adherence to Egyptian traditions, Cleopatra was also open to influences from other cultures, notably the Greek. This fusion of Egyptian and Hellenistic elements led to a unique cultural synthesis that was evident in the art, architecture, and coinage of her time. Today, we can take inspiration from her approach by being open to diverse cultural expressions and integrating them creatively into our own lives and work.

Art as a Medium of Personal and Political Expression: Cleopatra used art to express personal values and political messages. Her commissioned works often depicted her in symbolic contexts that conveyed her political messages subtly and effectively to her subjects and rivals. In our times, we too can use art to express our personal identity or social and political beliefs, utilizing creative outlets as powerful tools for communication and influence.

Meditative Practice: Art Appreciation Meditation

As we explore the impact of art in Cleopatra's life, let us engage in a meditative practice to deepen our appreciation of art and its influence on our personal development.

Choose a piece of art that resonates with you. It could be a painting, sculpture, piece of music, or even a beautifully designed building. Sit in a comfortable position in a quiet space where you can contemplate this art without interruption.

Close your eyes and take three deep breaths. With each exhale, release any tension you are holding in your body.

Now, open your eyes and focus on the art. Observe it carefully. Notice the colors, shapes, textures, or sounds. Imagine stepping into the artwork, becoming part of its environment, interacting with its forms and characters.

Reflect on what this piece of art expresses. What emotions does it evoke? What ideas or messages does it convey? Try to connect with the artist's intention, feeling the emotions they might have felt during its creation.

Think about how this art relates to your own life. Are there qualities or messages within the art that you can embody in your daily experiences? Visualize yourself integrating these elements into your life, enhancing your personal and professional interactions.

Take a few more deep breaths. With each inhale, imagine drawing in the beauty and inspiration from the art. With each exhale, imagine spreading this beauty and inspiration into the world around you.

Slowly bring your meditation to a close. Consider writing down any insights or feelings that arose during this meditation. How might you apply this newfound appreciation and understanding of art in your life?

Embracing the Cleopatra Effect through Arts

Cleopatra's legacy teaches us that art is not just a form of personal or aesthetic enjoyment but a profound tool for communication, influence, and self-expression. By incorporating art into our lives, we embrace a more holistic approach to personal development and interpersonal relations, just as Cleopatra did centuries ago. Whether through creating, patronizing, or simply appreciating art, we can enhance our own cultural footprint and continue the legacy of using beauty and creativity to impact our world.

Chapter 20: The Modern Cleopatra

Cleopatra VII, the last Pharaoh of Egypt, stands as a towering figure not just in the annals of history but as an emblem of power, intelligence, and charm that transcends centuries. Her legacy, shaped by both her formidable intellect and her dynamic personality, offers timeless lessons that can be adapted to the complexities of modern life. In this final chapter, we bridge the gap between ancient strategies and contemporary applications, helping you harness Cleopatra's enduring wisdom to navigate today's challenges and opportunities. By embodying the spirit of Cleopatra, you can cultivate a life of influence, resilience, and beauty.

Embracing Your Inner Ruler

Cleopatra was not merely born into power; she cultivated it through astute political acumen and relentless determination. Today's "Modern Cleopatra" can channel this same essence by taking command of her personal and professional realms. Leadership today demands more than authority; it requires empathy, adaptability, and the ability to inspire others. Like Cleopatra, who aligned with powerful counterparts to amplify her influence, you too can forge strategic alliances. Networking, mentoring, and collaborative ventures are the modern equivalents of Cleopatra's alliances with Julius Caesar and Mark Antony. Remember, every interaction is an opportunity to build your kingdom, whether that kingdom is your workplace, your community, or your field of expertise.

Cultivating Charisma and Influence

Cleopatra's charisma is legendary, turning enemies into allies and commanding respect across the political landscapes of Egypt and Rome. Charisma, however, was not merely a gift but a cultivated art. You can develop your charisma by being genuinely interested in others, listening actively, and communicating with passion and clarity. Cleopatra often wore striking garments and iconic makeup not just for beauty, but as a display of power and confidence. Similarly, consider how your personal style and presentation can enhance your presence in any room you enter. By embodying confidence and respect, you harness the power to influence.

Prioritizing Intellectual Growth

The commitment to intellectual growth was central to Cleopatra's rule. She was educated by philosophers and was known for her sharp intellect and ability to speak multiple languages. In the modern world, continual learning is just as crucial. Embrace a wide range of subjects, learn new skills, and challenge your mind regularly. This can be through formal education, self-study, or diverse experiences. Intellectual agility will allow you to navigate complex situations and innovate in ways that others might not foresee.

Nurturing Health and Beauty

Cleopatra understood the link between appearance and perception. Her beauty rituals, such as baths in milk and honey, were as much about self-care as they were about maintaining a persona. In today's fast-paced world, self-care is essential. It's not just about looking good but feeling your best. Integrating wellness practices into your daily routine—like mindfulness meditation, yoga, or even the modern-day equivalents of Cleopatra's baths (think spa days or skincare routines)—can enhance your physical and mental health.

The Art of Love and Relationships

Cleopatra's relationships were not just romantic; they were strategic alliances that helped stabilize and expand her empire. In the modern context, while love may not directly influence political realms, it still plays a crucial role in personal happiness and stability. Viewing relationships through the lens of mutual growth and support can lead to more fulfilling interactions. Communicate openly, set boundaries, and nurture the connections that enrich your life.

Building Resilience in Adversity

Cleopatra faced immense challenges during her reign—from political opposition to personal betrayal. Yet, she remained resilient, adapting to new threats and continually striving to reclaim her power. Today, resilience is just as crucial. Life's inevitable challenges, whether personal setbacks, professional obstacles, or broader societal issues, require a robust mental and emotional approach. Learn from failures, adapt to changes, and never lose sight of your goals, just as Cleopatra never did.

Leaving a Lasting Legacy

Lastly, consider what legacy you wish to leave behind. Cleopatra's story is still told thousands of years later because she lived with intention and impact. What impact do you want to have on your world? Whether it's through your career, your philanthropic efforts, or your role in your family or community, think about how you can make a lasting difference.

Meditation: Integrating the Spirit of Cleopatra

Let us conclude with a meditative practice to integrate the spirit of Cleopatra into your modern life. Find a quiet space and close your eyes. Breathe deeply and envision yourself walking through the bustling streets of ancient Alexandria. Feel the warm breeze and hear the mix of Greek and Egyptian spoken in the market.

Now, see yourself stepping into Cleopatra's palace, walking through its grand halls adorned with exquisite paintings and sculptures. Approach the throne, and see Cleopatra there, a figure of power and poise. She invites you to sit beside her.

As you sit, Cleopatra shares her wisdom on leadership, charisma, and resilience. With each word, you feel a sense of empowerment and clarity about your path. She hands you a golden ankh, symbolizing life and eternal wisdom.

Hold this symbol close to your heart, and slowly bring your awareness back to the present. Open your eyes, carrying with you the strength and wisdom of Cleopatra, ready to apply her timeless lessons to your modern life.

By channeling the qualities that made Cleopatra a legend, you are poised to become a modern-day Cleopatra, leading with wisdom, grace, and influence in every area of your life.

Made in the USA
Columbia, SC
13 November 2024

46428931R00059